EASY TAX PRO 2021

Easy Tax Workbook for Preparing
Your 2020 Tax Returns

Easy forms and checklists to give your tax preparer to get the smallest tax bill and largest refund.

*If this book helps you please
post a review on Amazon.*

INTRODUCTION

Most people don't want to become tax experts. They want an easy way to get their taxes filed with the smallest possible tax bill and the biggest possible refund.

This workbook for personal tax returns includes a worksheets for small businesses that use Schedule C

This workbook is all that 95% of taxpayers need to gather the documents and information to provide their tax preparers so he/she can do the best job possible for you.

The EASY Way to Get Prepared is the Easy Tax Pro Way!

There is a lot to know about tax law, but you don't need to know it all. Your tax preparer will use this information to ask questions needed.

In my tax preparation office, my clients have a 15-minute chat with me before I prepare their taxes. The chat involves the same questions in this workbook. Many of my clients tell me they now enjoy tax time.

◆ ◆ ◆

**Your tax preparer will be HAPPY to see you
when you arrive with this workbook!**

◆ ◆ ◆

IMPORTANT

This workbook is **NOT** to teach you how to do your own tax return. It is to prepare yourself to present your material to your tax preparer.

If you want to **learn to prepare tax returns**, this is **NOT** the book for you.

IF you do NOT want to figure out Schedule A, Schedule C, 1099-R, to itemize or not to itemize, but YOU DO want your tax preparer to do a BETTER job for you, then this workbook **IS FOR YOU**.

CONTENTS

Easy Tax Pro 2021   1

Introduction   2

IMPORTANT   5

A bizarre 2020   9

Get started   11

Essential Information   13

Dependent #1   16

Dependent #2   18

Dependent #3   20

Dependent #4   22

Dependent #5   24

Dependent #6   26

Dependent #7   28

Dependent #8   30

Earned Income Credit (EIC)   32

Child Tax Credit   34

Other Dependent Credit   35

Charity   36

Business Owner Income   37

Schedule C #1   38

Schedule C #2   41

Schedule C #3   44

Schedule C #4   47

Schedule C #5   50

Schedule C #6   53

Schedule C #7   56

Schedule C #8   59

Stimulus check FAQ   62

S-Corporation Questions   68

Easy Payroll Setup   73

Easy Way to Become Taxed as an S-Corporation   75

Employee or Independent Contractor?   78

Solve IRS Problems Cheap   81

About the Author   83

A BIZARRE 2020

What a bizarre year 2020 has been. As I prepared the first tax returns in January, neither I nor my clients expected this to be a time unlike any in our life, even the old people.

This year, my clients asked new questions. For example, my self-employed clients wanted to learn how to draw unemployment compensation. Self-employed people had never received unemployment compensation before, so it was a new territory for everyone, including the state government.

I considered telling them it wasn't my duty, but I wanted to be of good service to my clients, so I investigated the matter.

Additional questions were about the stimulus check. I helped my clients with these questions once the government disclosed the answers, which was painful to find.

New Stimulus Check Section.

This year I have added a stimulus check information section. People ask me if they can get one. Many wonder if they must pay it back or pay income tax on it.

New S-Corporation Advice Section.

I have added a new section about if you should have your small business taxed as an S-Corporation.

Previous tax preparers had not advised several of my new clients on the matter. In those cases, I brought it to their attention.

New Fix Irs Problems Section.

I get so mad when people pay out $5,000 or more to fix IRS tax problems when the problems could be solved inexpensively. I have included a section on how to solve your IRS tax problems.

Hire Employees Or Independent Contractors Section.

Many of my business owner clients wonder which is better. I include a section here so you will know.

GET STARTED

Let's Begin With Your Types Of Income

Below is a list of common documents you receive to show how much income you have earned. Write how many you have of each form on the line next to the form.

_____ W2 (From your employer)

_____ 1099-Misc (Independent contractor)

_____ 1099-R (Retirement income)

_____ 1099-DIV (Dividend income)

_____ 1099-INT (Interest Income)

_____ 1099-G (Government payments)

_____ 1099-SSA (Social Security income)

_____ W2G (Gambling income)

_____ 1098-T (Education credits)

_____ 1098-E (Student loan interest)

_____ 1099-B (Capital Gains)

_____ K-1,

What type K-1? _____

Other income documents _____

_____

ESSENTIAL INFORMATION

What is your first, last, and middle initial?

_____

What is your spouse's first, last, and middle initial?

_____

What is your date of birth?

_____

What is your spouse's date of birth?

_____

What is your occupation?

_____

What is your spouse's occupation?

_____

Are you married?   YES   NO

If you are married you should always have your tax preparer compare MFS (Married Filing Separately) or MFJ (Married Filing Jointly). Even though it was most advantageous for you to file MFS or MFJ one year does not mean it will be the next year.

If you are married is there a reason you MUST file MFS?

YES   NO

Did your spouse pass away within the last two years?

YES   NO

Did you move to a new residence in 2020?

YES   NO

Do you have assets or money in a foreign country?

YES   NO

Do you have your identification, such as drivers license, passport, or state ID?

YES   NO

If you want direct deposit from the IRS for your refund do you have your checking account number and routing number?

YES   NO

Did you contribute to an IRA in 2020?   YES   NO

Did you have a HSA for 2020?   YES   NO

Did you pay estimated taxes for 2020?   YES   NO

STIMULUS CHECKS

Did you get your stimulus checks?   YES   NO

Depending on your income, you should have got $1,200 each for you and your spouse, and $500 for every dependent age 16 or under.

If not, be sure your tax preparer gives you the credit for it on your tax return.

DEPENDENT #1

If you have dependents other than yourself or your spouse make sure you have the following information. You may write the information on this page or bring the information on other pages.

First, Middle, Last Name:

_____

Social Security #: _____

Birthday: _____

Relationship: _____

If this dependent was under the age of 13 as of 12/31/2020 you may be able to deduct child care expenses.

Child Care Expenses: $_____

Child Care Provider Name:

_____

Child Care Provider SS# or EIN#:

_____

Child Care Provider Address:

_____

Did this dependent live with you more than half of the year and did you provide more than half of the support?

YES   NO

Can this dependent be claimed as a dependent on anyone else's federal income tax return?

YES   NO

Do you have a form 8867 for this dependent?

YES   NO

DEPENDENT #2

If you have dependents other than yourself or your spouse make sure you have the following information. You may write the information on this page or bring the information on other pages.

First, Middle, Last Name:

_____

Social Security #: _____

Birthday: _____

Relationship: _____

If this dependent was under the age of 13 as of 12/31/2020 you may be able to deduct child care expenses.

Child Care Expenses: $_____

Child Care Provider Name:

_____

Child Care Provider SS# or EIN#:

_____

Child Care Provider Address:

_____

Did this dependent live with you more than half of the year and did you provide more than half of the support?

    YES   NO

Can this dependent be claimed as a dependent on anyone else's federal income tax return?

    YES   NO

Do you have a form 8867 for this dependent?

    YES   NO

DEPENDENT #3

If you have dependents other than yourself or your spouse make sure you have the following information. You may write the information on this page or bring the information on other pages.

First, Middle, Last Name:

_____

Social Security #: _____

Birthday: _____

Relationship: _____

If this dependent was under the age of 13 as of 12/31/2020 you may be able to deduct child care expenses.

Child Care Expenses: $_____

Child Care Provider Name:

_____

Child Care Provider SS# or EIN#:

_____

Child Care Provider Address:

_____

Did this dependent live with you more than half of the year and did you provide more than half of the support?

YES   NO

Can this dependent be claimed as a dependent on anyone else's federal income tax return?

YES   NO

Do you have a form 8867 for this dependent?

YES   NO

DEPENDENT #4

If you have dependents other than yourself or your spouse make sure you have the following information. You may write the information on this page or bring the information on other pages.

First, Middle, Last Name:

_____

Social Security #: _____

Birthday: _____

Relationship: _____

If this dependent was under the age of 13 as of 12/31/2020 you may be able to deduct child care expenses.

Child Care Expenses: $_____

Child Care Provider Name:

_____

Child Care Provider SS# or EIN#:

_____

Child Care Provider Address:

_____

Did this dependent live with you more than half of the year and did you provide more than half of the support?

    YES   NO

Can this dependent be claimed as a dependent on anyone else's federal income tax return?

    YES   NO

Do you have a form 8867 for this dependent?

    YES   NO

DEPENDENT #5

If you have dependents other than yourself or your spouse make sure you have the following information. You may write the information on this page or bring the information on other pages.

First, Middle, Last Name:

_____

Social Security #: _____

Birthday: _____

Relationship: _____

If this dependent was under the age of 13 as of 12/31/2020 you may be able to deduct child care expenses.

Child Care Expenses: $_____

Child Care Provider Name:

_____

Child Care Provider SS# or EIN#:

_____

Child Care Provider Address:

_____

Did this dependent live with you more than half of the year and did you provide more than half of the support?

YES   NO

Can this dependent be claimed as a dependent on anyone else's federal income tax return?

YES   NO

Do you have a form 8867 for this dependent?

YES   NO

DEPENDENT #6

If you have dependents other than yourself or your spouse make sure you have the following information. You may write the information on this page or bring the information on other pages.

First, Middle, Last Name:

_____

Social Security #: _____

Birthday: _____

Relationship: _____

If this dependent was under the age of 13 as of 12/31/2020 you may be able to deduct child care expenses.

Child Care Expenses: $_____

Child Care Provider Name:

_____

Child Care Provider SS# or EIN#:

_____

Child Care Provider Address:

_____

Did this dependent live with you more than half of the year and did you provide more than half of the support?

YES   NO

Can this dependent be claimed as a dependent on anyone else's federal income tax return?

YES   NO

Do you have a form 8867 for this dependent?

YES   NO

DEPENDENT #7

If you have dependents other than yourself or your spouse make sure you have the following information. You may write the information on this page or bring the information on other pages.

First, Middle, Last Name:

_____

Social Security #: _____

Birthday: _____

Relationship: _____

If this dependent was under the age of 13 as of 12/31/2020 you may be able to deduct child care expenses.

Child Care Expenses: $_____

Child Care Provider Name:

_____

Child Care Provider SS# or EIN#:

_____

Child Care Provider Address:

_____

Did this dependent live with you more than half of the year and did you provide more than half of the support?

YES　NO

Can this dependent be claimed as a dependent on anyone else's federal income tax return?

YES　NO

Do you have a form 8867 for this dependent?

YES　NO

DEPENDENT #8

If you have dependents other than yourself or your spouse make sure you have the following information. You may write the information on this page or bring the information on other pages.

First, Middle, Last Name:

_____

Social Security #: _____

Birthday: _____

Relationship: _____

If this dependent was under the age of 13 as of 12/31/2020 you may be able to deduct child care expenses.

Child Care Expenses: $_____

Child Care Provider Name:

_____

Child Care Provider SS# or EIN#:

_____

Child Care Provider Address:

_____

Did this dependent live with you more than half of the year and did you provide more than half of the support?

YES   NO

Can this dependent be claimed as a dependent on anyone else's federal income tax return?

YES   NO

Do you have a form 8867 for this dependent?

YES   NO

EARNED INCOME CREDIT (EIC)

Will you be claiming the EIC?

YES   NO   I DON'T KNOW

Qualifying Children Claimed

If filing	Zero	One	Two	Three
Single, Head of Household, or Widowed	$15,820	$41,756	$47,440	$50,954
Married Filing Jointly	$21,710	$47,646	$53,330	$56,844

Investment Income Limit
Investment income must be $3,650 or less for the year.

Maximum Credit Amounts
The maximum amount of credit for Tax Year 2020 is:

- $6,660 with three or more qualifying children
- $5,920 with two qualifying children
- $3,584 with one qualifying child
- $538 with no qualifying children.

If you are claiming the EIC you will need to show proof of residence for your children. This can be medical records, school records, healthcare provider statement, childcare provider records, placement agency statement, social services records or statement, place of worship statement, Indian tribal official statement, employer statement, or landlord or property management statement.

Do you have one of these documents? YES   NO

CHILD TAX CREDIT

The child needs to be under age 17 as of 12/31/2020

Will you be claiming the Child Tax Credit?

   YES   NO   I DON'T KNOW

If you are claiming the Child Tax Credit you will need to show proof of residence for your children. This can be medical records, school records, healthcare provider statement, childcare provider records, placement agency statement, social services records or statement, place of worship statement, Indian tribal official statement, employer statement, or landlord or property management statement.

Do you have one of these documents? YES   NO

OTHER DEPENDENT CREDIT

The dependent needs to be age 17 or over as of 12/31/20

Will you be claiming the Other Dependent Credit?

   YES   NO   I DON'T KNOW

If you are claiming the Other Dependent Credit Credit you will need to show proof of residence for your children. This can be medical records, school records, healthcare provider statement, childcare provider records, placement agency statement, social services records or statement, place of worship statement, Indian tribal official statement, employer statement, or landlord or property management statement.

Do you have one of these documents? YES   NO

CHARITY

Did you donate money to charity in 2020?

YES   NO

If yes, how much: $_____

Did you donate goods, furniture, clothing, etc to charity in 2020?

YES   NO

If yes, what was the value: $_____

Do you have receipts or proof of payment to the charities?

YES   NO

Do you have mileage for charity?

YES   NO

If yes, how many miles? _____

BUSINESS OWNER INCOME

If you have a business or 1099-Misc income, you need to use this page.

Did you earn income from Uber or Lyft?

YES   NO

If yes, you need to use the Schedule C page.

Did you operate your business as a sole proprietorship?

YES   NO

If yes, you need to use the Schedule C page.

If no, you need to use a tax form not included in this guide.

If you have an LLC, did you operate your business as a sole proprietorship?

YES   NO

If yes, you need to use the Schedule C page.

If no, you need to use a tax form not included in this guide.

SCHEDULE C #1

What is the name of your business?

_____

Is this business owned by the taxpayer or spouse?

Taxpayer   Spouse

What is your product or service?

_____

What is your business address?

_____

Do you have an Employment Identification Number (EIN) for your business?

Yes, this is the number: _____

If no, you will use your social security number.

Did you use a home office?

YES   NO

If yes, what is the square footage of your home?

_____

If yes, what is the square footage of your office?

_____

If yes, how much did you spend on utilities and rent for your home in 2020?

_____

Did you use a vehicle for this business?

YES   NO

If yes, what is the make and year of your vehicle?

_____

What date did you put your vehicle into service for this business? (Does not have to be exact).

_____

Was your vehicle available for personal use during off-duty hours?

YES   NO

Did you have another vehicle available for personal use?

YES   NO

Do you have a mileage log?

YES   NO

If no, do you have records of gas purchases to calculate mileage? This should include a regular schedule of travel.

YES   NO

If you drove for Uber or Lyft they report your mileage while logged into the app on your K-1. MAKE SURE your tax preparer adds mileage for when you had your app turned off.

What is the mileage for business?

_____

What is the mileage for personal or commuting?

_____

SCHEDULE C #2

What is the name of your business?

_____

Is this business owned by the taxpayer or spouse?

Taxpayer   Spouse

What is your product or service?

_____

What is your business address?

_____

Do you have an Employment Identification Number (EIN) for your business?

Yes, this is the number: _____

If no, you will use your social security number.

Did you use a home office?

YES   NO

If yes, what is the square footage of your home?

_____

If yes, what is the square footage of your office?

_____

If yes, how much did you spend on utilities and rent for your home in 2020?

_____

Did you use a vehicle for this business?

YES   NO

If yes, what is the make and year of your vehicle?

_____

What date did you put your vehicle into service for this business? (Does not have to be exact).

_____

Was your vehicle available for personal use during off-duty hours?

YES   NO

Did you have another vehicle available for personal use?

YES   NO

Do you have a mileage log?

YES   NO

If no, do you have records of gas purchases to calculate mileage? This should include a regular schedule of travel.

YES   NO

If you drove for Uber or Lyft they report your mileage while logged into the app on your K-1. MAKE SURE your tax preparer adds mileage for when you had your app turned off.

What is the mileage for business?

_____

What is the mileage for personal or commuting?

_____

SCHEDULE C #3

What is the name of your business?

_____

Is this business owned by the taxpayer or spouse?

Taxpayer   Spouse

What is your product or service?

_____

What is your business address?

_____

Do you have an Employment Identification Number (EIN) for your business?

Yes, this is the number: _____

If no, you will use your social security number.

Did you use a home office?

YES   NO

If yes, what is the square footage of your home?

_____

If yes, what is the square footage of your office?

_____

If yes, how much did you spend on utilities and rent for your home in 2020?

_____

Did you use a vehicle for this business?

YES   NO

If yes, what is the make and year of your vehicle?

_____

What date did you put your vehicle into service for this business? (Does not have to be exact).

_____

Was your vehicle available for personal use during off-duty hours?

YES   NO

Did you have another vehicle available for personal use?

YES   NO

Do you have a mileage log?

YES   NO

If no, do you have records of gas purchases to calculate mileage? This should include a regular schedule of travel.

YES   NO

If you drove for Uber or Lyft they report your mileage while logged into the app on your K-1. MAKE SURE your tax preparer adds mileage for when you had your app turned off.

What is the mileage for business?

_____

What is the mileage for personal or commuting?

_____

SCHEDULE C #4

What is the name of your business?

_____

Is this business owned by the taxpayer or spouse?

Taxpayer Spouse

What is your product or service?

_____

What is your business address?

_____

Do you have an Employment Identification Number (EIN) for your business?

Yes, this is the number: _____

If no, you will use your social security number.

Did you use a home office?

YES   NO

If yes, what is the square footage of your home?

_____

If yes, what is the square footage of your office?

_____

If yes, how much did you spend on utilities and rent for your home in 2020?

_____

Did you use a vehicle for this business?

YES   NO

If yes, what is the make and year of your vehicle?

_____

What date did you put your vehicle into service for this business? (Does not have to be exact).

_____

Was your vehicle available for personal use during off-duty hours?

YES   NO

Did you have another vehicle available for personal use?

YES   NO

Do you have a mileage log?

YES   NO

If no, do you have records of gas purchases to calculate mileage? This should include a regular schedule of travel.

YES   NO

If you drove for Uber or Lyft they report your mileage while logged into the app on your K-1. MAKE SURE your tax preparer adds mileage for when you had your app turned off.

What is the mileage for business?

_____

What is the mileage for personal or commuting?

_____

49

SCHEDULE C #5

What is the name of your business?

_____

Is this business owned by the taxpayer or spouse?

Taxpayer   Spouse

What is your product or service?

_____

What is your business address?

_____

Do you have an Employment Identification Number (EIN) for your business?

Yes, this is the number: _____

If no, you will use your social security number.

Did you use a home office?

YES   NO

If yes, what is the square footage of your home?

_____

If yes, what is the square footage of your office?

_____

If yes, how much did you spend on utilities and rent for your home in 2020?

_____

Did you use a vehicle for this business?

YES   NO

If yes, what is the make and year of your vehicle?

_____

What date did you put your vehicle into service for this business? (Does not have to be exact).

_____

Was your vehicle available for personal use during off-duty hours?

YES   NO

Did you have another vehicle available for personal use?

YES   NO

Do you have a mileage log?

YES   NO

If no, do you have records of gas purchases to calculate mileage? This should include a regular schedule of travel.

YES   NO

If you drove for Uber or Lyft they report your mileage while logged into the app on your K-1. MAKE SURE your tax preparer adds mileage for when you had your app turned off.

What is the mileage for business?

_____

What is the mileage for personal or commuting?

_____

SCHEDULE C #6

What is the name of your business?

_____

Is this business owned by the taxpayer or spouse?

Taxpayer   Spouse

What is your product or service?

_____

What is your business address?

_____

Do you have an Employment Identification Number (EIN) for your business?

Yes, this is the number: _____

If no, you will use your social security number.

Did you use a home office?

YES   NO

If yes, what is the square footage of your home?

_____

If yes, what is the square footage of your office?

_____

If yes, how much did you spend on utilities and rent for your home in 2020?

_____

Did you use a vehicle for this business?

YES   NO

If yes, what is the make and year of your vehicle?

_____

What date did you put your vehicle into service for this business? (Does not have to be exact).

_____

Was your vehicle available for personal use during off-duty hours?

YES   NO

Did you have another vehicle available for personal use?

YES   NO

Do you have a mileage log?

YES   NO

If no, do you have records of gas purchases to calculate mileage? This should include a regular schedule of travel.

YES   NO

If you drove for Uber or Lyft they report your mileage while logged into the app on your K-1. MAKE SURE your tax preparer adds mileage for when you had your app turned off.

What is the mileage for business?

_____

What is the mileage for personal or commuting?

_____

SCHEDULE C #7

What is the name of your business?

_____

Is this business owned by the taxpayer or spouse?

Taxpayer   Spouse

What is your product or service?

_____

What is your business address?

_____

Do you have an Employment Identification Number (EIN) for your business?

Yes, this is the number: _____

If no, you will use your social security number.

Did you use a home office?

YES   NO

If yes, what is the square footage of your home?

_____

If yes, what is the square footage of your office?

_____

If yes, how much did you spend on utilities and rent for your home in 2020?

_____

Did you use a vehicle for this business?

YES   NO

If yes, what is the make and year of your vehicle?

_____

What date did you put your vehicle into service for this business? (Does not have to be exact).

_____

Was your vehicle available for personal use during off-duty hours?

YES   NO

Did you have another vehicle available for personal use?

YES   NO

Do you have a mileage log?

YES   NO

If no, do you have records of gas purchases to calculate mileage? This should include a regular schedule of travel.

YES   NO

If you drove for Uber or Lyft they report your mileage while logged into the app on your K-1. MAKE SURE your tax preparer adds mileage for when you had your app turned off.

What is the mileage for business?

_____

What is the mileage for personal or commuting?

_____

SCHEDULE C #8

What is the name of your business?

_____

Is this business owned by the taxpayer or spouse?

Taxpayer Spouse

What is your product or service?

_____

What is your business address?

_____

Do you have an Employment Identification Number (EIN) for your business?

Yes, this is the number: _____

If no, you will use your social security number.

Did you use a home office?

YES   NO

If yes, what is the square footage of your home?

_____

If yes, what is the square footage of your office?

_____

If yes, how much did you spend on utilities and rent for your home in 2020?

_____

Did you use a vehicle for this business?

YES   NO

If yes, what is the make and year of your vehicle?

_____

What date did you put your vehicle into service for this business? (Does not have to be exact).

_____

Was your vehicle available for personal use during off-duty hours?

YES   NO

Did you have another vehicle available for personal use?

YES   NO

Do you have a mileage log?

YES   NO

If no, do you have records of gas purchases to calculate mileage? This should include a regular schedule of travel.

YES   NO

If you drove for Uber or Lyft they report your mileage while logged into the app on your K-1. MAKE SURE your tax preparer adds mileage for when you had your app turned off.

What is the mileage for business?

_____

What is the mileage for personal or commuting?

_____

STIMULUS CHECK FAQ

This year, the government created a tax credit unlike any before. They called it the stimulus check.

My client's reaction to the stimulus check was like the **frenzy of bees escaping their beehive eaten by a bear.** The IRS was not prepared to mail out the checks. There were glitches that caused pain in the lives of my clients, but it's expected when you consider the monumental task entrusted to them.

In March of this year, when the COVID-19 Pandemic began, anyone who had not reported taxes in 2017 or 2018 **would not** get a stimulus check. The IRS promised a solution and after several weeks they added a form for non-filers to IRS.gov. This did not apply to individuals receiving Social Security, they were the first group to get stimulus checks.

The non-filers' return was a godsend, but a glitch in the system came to light later in the tax season. Frequently, when I went to E-file a tax return, I got an error message from the IRS saying my client had previously filed their tax return. My client knew they hadn't filed it. I knew they hadn't if they were repeat clients, **unless they had been sneaking around in a dark bar behind my back with another tax preparer.**

Eventually, the IRS reported that in some cases, their system accidentally marked that taxpayers had already filed their tax return when they used the non-filers form. For those people, we had to mail in their tax return. It is a much slower process to get a tax refund by mail than by e-file. This year, it was even worse because the IRS offices had been closed down for many weeks and they had processed no paper returns. Over **five million returns had piled up** on the desks of the IRS agents while they were home, protecting themselves from COVID-19.

I can just imagine those poor IRS employees when they first returned to their offices with piles of tax returns resembling the **Swiss Alps**. I heard some agents had to use **snow shovels just to recover their desks**.

Question: Do I Get My Stimulus Check If I Owe Back Taxes?

My phone rang., it alerted me it was one of my tax client as Jane's name popped up.

"Hello, Jane." I said.

"You always throw me off when you call me by name!" Jane said.

"Yeah, technology is amazing, huh? What can I do for you?"

"Tim, I owe back taxes, as you know, and I'm wondering if I will get the stimulus check."

"Yes, Jane. You will still get the stimulus check. The government is not holding it because of back taxes owed."

"Thank you, Tim will be in to see you shortly."
"Great, always happy to have you back, Jane!"

Question: Do I Get My Stimulus Check If I Owe Back Child Support?

My phone rings again. This time it is Bob.

"Hey Bob, how are you doing?"

"Hi Tim. I'm wondering if I'm going to get the stimulus check."

"Everybody will get it even if they haven't filed taxes. Unless, that is, if you owe back child tax support."

"Oh, that's terrible. I'm making payments on back child support to catch up. Will that help?"

"No, the only case that they're not issuing stimulus checks is for people who owe back child support, even if you're in an arrangement making payments. I'm very sorry."

"OK. Darn. I was hoping I would get it. Well, will be in to see you soon."

"Sorry that it's bad news for you, Bob, but I look forward to seeing you in here. Have a great day."

Question: What If We Qualified For A Stimulus Check For Our Dependents But Did Not Receive It?

My phone buzzed, flashing is Jamie's name, another of my Tax Clients.

"Hello Jamie, how are you doing today?"

"I'm doing good, Tim. Thanks for answering the phone so fast."

"You're welcome."

"Tim, I got my stimulus check for me and my husband. $2400, but we didn't get the $500 for our two children. What can we do about that?"

"That's not a problem. When we file your taxes for 2020, I will add it to your refund."

"Thank you very much, Tim."

"You're welcome, Jamie. Have a nice day."

Question: What If I Did Not Get Any Stimulus Check?

My phone rang again. I guessed there would not be time for my lunch. Jules' name popped up on my phone.

"Hi Jules, how's it going?"

"Hi Tim. I hate to bother you, but I never got my stimulus check. What can I do about it?"

"Well, since you file taxes every year, you should've got it. If you don't have it by the time we file your taxes, you'll get it as a refund on your tax return."

"Oh Thank You Tim, Very Much. Do I Get A Stimulus Check For My Children?"

"Yes, if they are 16 or under and are not claimed as a dependent on someone else's tax return."

"Tim, You Know My Son, Jeremy, Is In College, Will He Get A Stimulus Check?"

"Jules, if he files "dependent of another" on his tax return, yes. If he chooses not to be your dependent you may lose out on $2,500 for his 1098-T."

"So, Jeremy can get $1,200 but we won't get $2,500 from his 1098-T? Will he get the $2,400?"

"With his income as a college student he will only get $1,000 instead of $2,500."

"This is confusing."

"I know. It comes down to either you will get $2,500 or Jeremy will get $2,200."

"Tim, Do I Have To Pay The Stimulus Checks Back?"

"You do not."

"What About Income Tax. Will It Increase My Taxable Income?"

"No Jules, you do not pay any income tax on the stimulus check."

"I appreciate your time, thank you.

"You're welcome, Jules. See you in the spring."

S-CORPORATION QUESTIONS

Question: Should You Have Your Business Taxed As An S-Corporation Instead Of As A Sole-Proprietor?

"Hello Tim." Shirley said as she strapped her face mask on while strolling in the door.

"Hello Shirley, it's nice to meet you. Come have a seat six feet away from my desk." I pulled my fog resistance face shield over my masked face. "Shirley, who did your taxes last year?"

"The same person for the last twenty years, but he retired."

"OK, I see you have a small business with a $30,000 profit. The IRS is taxing you as a sole-proprietor. How long have you had this business?"

"I've been running it for 15 years now."

"How many years did you have at least $10,000 in profit?"

"Starting in year four, all of them. I've had outstanding success."

"Yes, I see you have, congratulations. You're an astute business owner. However, I want the IRS to tax you differently for next year. You could pay a lot less in taxes."

"How so?" Shirley leaned forward.

"Well, for example, this year if the IRS had taxed you as an S-corporation instead of a sole-proprietor **you would have saved $3000.**"

"Why wasn't my tax guy before doing that?"

"I don't have an answer for you on that."

"Oh my God, I've probably been overpaying for 15 years."

"Yep, you sure were. But we're going to fix it now."

This conversation with Shirley was a common conversation I had in 2020 with my small business clients. I recognized how often tax preparers do not properly advise their clients.

If you have a small business and are currently operating it as a sole-proprietor, you may wonder if you should instead be operating as a corporation.

Even if you have an LLC, you still may operate as a sole-proprietor. **An LLC is like Tofu. It takes on the flavor of any ingredient you mix with it.** You can operate an LLC as a sole-proprietor, C-corporation, S-corporation or partnership. I'm only going to talk about the two options of sole-proprietor and S-corporation.

If You Are Making A Profit Of More Than $10,000 Per Year, It Will Benefit You To Ask The Irs To Tax

You As An S-Corporation.

Question: Is There An Easier Way To Pay Less Taxes Like An S-Corporation Without Having To Be An S-Corporation And Save On Expensive Attorney Fees And Annual Fees?

I'm not telling you to create an S-Corporation. There's nothing wrong with that, but if you do, you're going to need to make sure you have an attorney involved to file annual reports for you.

However, at least in the state of Ohio, if you have an LLC and don't take any of the optional stuff when setting it up, there are no annual papers to file. It's much easier to operate an LLC than a regular corporation.

If you have an LLC, you can ask the IRS to tax you as an S-Corporation instead of as a sole-proprietor. To do this, there is a simple form you or your tax preparer can mail or fax to the IRS. It's a simple form, number XXXXX which you can get by searching IRS.gov.

You must then wait for the IRS to give approval for you to be taxed as an S-Corporation. The IRS so far has never refused my clients, so I doubt you will be.

So, How Does Operating As An S-Corporation Help You?

Let's take the example of somebody with a business that made a profit of $60,000. If you're operating as a sole-proprietor, you have to pay self-employment taxes in most cases on all $60,000. There are situations where that is not true, but usually it's because you've already made $130,000 or more than a single person or $260,000 as a married couple on your W-2. You only have to pay Social Security on the first $130,000 of your total income. However, you still continue to pay Medicare on your earned wages no matter how much you make.

Let's assume your W-2 income between you and your spouse is $50,000. In this case, you must pay the self-employment tax on all of the $60,000 profit for the business.

Self-employment tax is just another name for Social Security and Medicare. When you're an employee, you see that in your W-2 and your paystub. But when you're self-employed as a sole-proprietor you have to pay the tax. This year, the self-employment tax is 15.3%. So, on a profit of $60,000, you will pay $9,180 in self-employment tax. This is in addition to any income tax you may have to pay.

But let's say you operate as an S-corporation. You do not have to pay self-employment tax on the company's profit. It is pass-through income to your personal taxes.

As an S-corporation, you will then need to pay yourself as an employee. The rule of thumb is to pay yourself about one-third of what your profit will be. If you expect to make a $50,000 profit then pay yourself $16,667 as an employee, or about $320 per week.

The rest of the $33,333 will flow through to your personal tax return. You will not need to pay self-employment tax on that $33,333.

I Bet I Know What You Are Thinking Now. Why Can't I Just Have All $50,000 Profit Flow Through And Pay Zero Self-Employment Taxes?

Am I right? Did you just think that?

Well, here is the reason. **The IRS does not like that.** They want you to pay some of your profit to yourself as an employee. What amount? They don't tell us. But from industry standards, it is to the best of my knowledge that the IRS has never complained about one-third of the profits paid to you as an employee.

So this means you do not have to pay self-employment tax on 2/3 of your $50,000 which is going to **save you $5,100** in self-employment tax.

EASY PAYROLL SETUP

I'm going to talk to you about the easiest way to pay yourself as an employee.

Unless you're already a payroll expert or have an accountant that can do your payroll for you, I strongly suggest that you use the **Square.com** payroll system. It is the easiest I have ever found. They will charge you $37 per month +5 dollars per employee.

Each week **estimate what a third of your profit will be** and pay that amount to yourself as an employee. For example, if you're making $1000 a week in profit, you're going to pay yourself as an employee for $333. All you need to do is log into your Square account and say pay me $333. Square takes care of everything else for you.

Each time you pay yourself Square withholds your federal income tax, Social Security, Medicare, state tax, school tax, local and city tax. The money is out of your bank account and you don't have to worry about it anymore.

At the appropriate time, Square will file all the tax forms and pay the taxes needed with all the particular government agencies.

It can be even simpler if you just want to do a set standard weekly check at $333. You don't have to log in every week. Square will automatically direct deposit your pay to your checking account.

At the end of the year, you'll get your W-2, which shows the Social

Security, Medicare, federal, state, and city withholding. The balance of the profit from your business will flow through to your 1040. On that income, you only have to pay your normal income tax, not self-employment tax.

EASY WAY TO BECOME TAXED AS AN S-CORPORATION

Here Are The Steps You Will Need To Do To Get To This Tax Benefit:

Number one, if you do not already have an LLC, you need to set one up. I've only worked with Ohio, which is very simple. **You go to the Ohio website to create an LLC. The fee is only $99.** If you are in another state, you may have to ask a local tax preparer to help you.

After you do that,you're going to need to **get your EIN number**, which is your employer identification number from the IRS. This is also very simple and you will get the number immediately if you have the letter given to you as a PDF instead of having it mailed to you. Go to the IRS.gov website and put EIN in the search box. It will take you to the page you need.

The next thing you must do is **get a withholding number from your state.** Not all states charge income tax, which makes it even easier for you. With Ohio, you can go onto the Ohio website and set up your employer withholding number.

In most states you must **set up unemployment.** Here in Ohio, that's also very simple. Here's the link to go do that. You will need your state charter number from your LLC, and the EIN number from the IRS. You may need to wait a couple days for the EIN to be in the system so other people can recognize it at the IRS.

A couple days after you received your EIN from the IRS, you'll want to **set up a checking account** for your LLC. If you already have an LLC and you already have a checking account, you can skip this step. If not, you need to take your LLC charter number and your EIN number to the bank to create a checking account.

When you're setting up your payroll inside of Square, Square will take the taxes and payroll from the business checking account. They will then direct deposit your net pay to your personal checking account.

If you're paying yourself $300 per week, you can expect about $330 taken from your business checking account. This is because of the extra taxes.

Once you have all the setup, you don't have to think about it anymore. It's a very simple solution.

Other benefits to getting a W-2 could be seen when you finance a car or go to the bank. I'm sure you've already figured out that **banks don't like self-employed people, but they sure do love employees.** That's never made sense to me because they assume the employee has a more steady job or income than the person who owns the business they are working for. If the business fails, the employees lose their jobs.

My phone rings and Elizabeth's name pops up.

Elizabeth, what can I help you with today?.

Tim, last year you told me if I thought I was going to make more than $10,000 in profit that you should help me get set up as an S-corporation. I can't believe it's happening during this Covid year, but I believe I'm actually going to hit $30,000 in profit this year.

Well, that's great to hear Elizabeth. Yes, I can certainly help you do all that. **It's odd you would call right now because I am writing about how to do this in my book.**

What a coincidence. I must get your book.

You don't need it because you got me.

Ha ha. I do have you, I'm grateful for that.

Well, come on in, it'll take a couple hours to go through the process. Hopefully, my book will help everybody who is not my client to decide if they need to have the IRS tax them as an S-corporation or not.

EMPLOYEE OR INDEPENDENT CONTRACTOR?

Should I Pay My Hired Help As Employees Or As Independent Contractors?

There are about 21 specific questions the IRS asks to determine if your workers should be an employee or independent contractor. But to be simple, it boils down to this.

If you tell your worker **when to show up for work, how to do his/ her job and provide tools for them,** then you should make them an employee.

It would be **safe to make them an independent contractor** if they work for other people besides you, they provide their own tools, they decide when to work, and how they are going to accomplish that work.

If the IRS finds you have been paying your workers as independent contractors when in fact they should have been employees, you could face **big fines**. In addition, **the IRS will force you to pay all the taxes that you should have withheld** from their paychecks, all the years you violated this rule.

Question: But Isn't It Expensive And Complicated To Pay My Workers As Employees As Compared To Independent Contractors?

Answer: First, let's talk about the expense. If you were to pay yourself $1000 as an employee and have taxes withheld, your total cost is about $1,075.

If you paid yourself $1,000 as a sole-proprietor, your cost is about $1,150. (Your profit plus self-employment tax).

So the simple answer is **it is NOT more expensive** to pay yourself as an employee.

But .... **is it too complicated?**

Answer: It could be. Or it could be easy.

You may already have someone who takes care of your payroll for you. If so, great! If not, **Square.com** has a payroll service, that is fantastically easy.

After you set up Square payroll with your EIN (Employer Identification Number), your state tax withholding ID, (if you pay your state taxes), your unemployment ID, and your personal and business checking account, there is very little for you to do.

Square will withhold federal, state, city, medicare, and social security taxes when they pay you. You don't need to worry about coming up with the money later.

Then when the time is right, Square will file all the tax forms and pay them.

Square will even give you your W-2 at the end of the year.

For this service, they charge $37 per month plus $5 per month per employee. If it is just you your fee is $42 total.

All you must do is log in each week and enter how much you want to be paid. If you don't want to do that, you can do it monthly. You can even set a certain amount to pay you every pay period and never log in.

SOLVE IRS PROBLEMS CHEAP

Is There A Way To Solve My Irs Tax Problems Without Hiring Firms On The Radio That Charge $5,000?

Answer: YES!

Based on conversations with my clients with tax problems, **90% of them only needed to file income tax returns and make a request to the IRS for a payment plan.** Many believed they would have to pay thousands of dollars to one of these tax-fix companies to get right with the IRS.

Before you request to set up a payment plan, you must have all your tax returns filed for at least the last six years. Usually filing the last six years of tax returns will make the IRS happy, but there are exceptions.

For individuals, if you owe less than $50,000 in combined tax, penalties, and interest, you can request a payment plan up to seventy-two months, (six years), at **3% interest**. That is much **cheaper than a credit card**.

If you owe more than $50,000 but less than $100,000 the longest payment plan available for you is six months.

If you operate your business as a sole-proprietor or you are an independent contractor, you will still file as an individual. If you have a business that operates otherwise other rules apply.

The form to apply for the payment plan is simple. You can find it and **apply online at IRS.gov.** Type in "**payment plan**" in the search box. You may also have your tax preparer fill out and e-file the request for the payment plan.

Question: What Is The Cost To Hire A Tax Preparer To Do This For Me?

Answer: It should only be the **normal cost for filing the tax returns** you are missing and maybe a few extra dollars to fill out the payment request form. If it is a lot more than that, find another tax preparer.

I hope this book has been of help to you. I love this system I have put together for my clients, and I believe you will also.

ABOUT THE AUTHOR

Timothy L. Drobnick Sr. has a very accomplished business history. He donates his time helping others start their own businesses in Gahanna, Ohio.

He opened Easy Tax Pro in a shopping center in December 2015 and has enjoyed great success and support from the local residents. His office is at:

Easy Tax Pro LLC
963 East Johnstown Road
Gahanna, Ohio 43230
1(614)477-5215

In 2018, he started preparing taxes nationwide with the help of capable and trained employees.

Tim has the AFSP from the IRS as do his employees. His name is listed on the official IRS website as having completed this training.

Tim's facebook is:
https://www.facebook.com/tim.drobnick.5

Tim's Email is:
Tim@EasyTaxPro.com

If this book has helped you please

post a review on Amazon.

Hicksville Public Library

169 Jerusalem Ave

Hicksville, NY 11801

Ph: 516-931-1417

Made in the USA
Middletown, DE
11 December 2020

27131661R00050